NEW BOOKS FOR NEW READERS

Phyllis MacAdam, *General Editor*

Kentucky Ghosts

William Lynwood Montell

THE UNIVERSITY PRESS OF KENTUCKY

Scholarly publisher for the Commonwealth,
serving Bellarmine University, Berea College, Centre
College of Kentucky, Eastern Kentucky University,
The Filson Historical Society, Georgetown College,
Kentucky Historical Society, Kentucky State University,
Morehead State University, Murray State University,
Northern Kentucky University, Transylvania University,
University of Kentucky, University of Louisville,
and Western Kentucky University.
All rights reserved.

Editorial and Sales Offices: The University Press of Kentucky
663 South Limestone Street, Lexington, Kentucky 40508-4008
www.kentuckypress.com

08 07 06 05 04   8 7 6 5 4

Library of Congress Cataloging-in-Publication Data

Montell, William Lynwood, 1931–
    Kentucky ghosts / William Lynwood Montell.
      p.   cm. — (New books for new readers)
    ISBN 0-8131-0909-4 (alk. paper) :
    1. Ghosts—Kentucky. 2. Tales—Kentucky. I. Title. II. Series.
GR110.K4M665   1994
398.25'09769—dc20   93-37211

This book is printed on acid-free recycled paper meeting
the requirements of the American National Standard
for Permanence of Paper for Printed Library Materials.

Manufactured in the United States of America

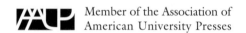

Member of the Association of
American University Presses

Contents

Foreword

The Kentucky Humanities Council began its New Books for New Readers project because Kentucky's adult literacy students want books that recognize their intelligence and experience while meeting their need for simplicity in writing. The first eight titles in the New Books for New Readers series have helped many adult students open a window on the wonderful world of literacy. At the same time, the New Books, with their plain language and compelling stories of Kentucky history and culture, have found a wider audience among accomplished readers of all ages who recognize a good read when they see one. As we publish the ninth New Book, we thank our authors and our readers, who together have proved that New Books and the humanities are for everyone.

This volume was made possible, in part, by the continuing assistance of the Scripps Howard Foundation through the *Kentucky Post* and through support from the Louisville *Courier-Journal*, the Moninger Schmidt Fund, and friends of the Kentucky Humanities Council. The co-sponsorship and assistance of the Kentucky Department for Libraries and Archives and the Kentucky Literacy Commission has been essential to our undertaking. We are also grateful for the advice and support provided to us by the University Press of Kentucky. All of these agencies share our commitment to the important role reading books plays in the lives of the people of our Commonwealth.

Virginia G. Smith, Executive Director
Kentucky Humanities Council

Acknowledgments

Many people have had a hand in producing a book by the time it appears in print. I wish to thank the Kentucky Humanities Council, the *Kentucky Post*, and the University Press of Kentucky for making the publication of this book possible. Phyllis MacAdam, cordinator of the New Books for New Readers Project, was especially helpful in providing content and editorial insight and assistance. Folklorist Trudy Balcom deserves a special note of thanks for helping me expand on the historical and cultural details necessary to make a good story even better. I wish also to thank Michelle Hunt, Warren County literacy coordinator, and all the new readers and their tutors who read and commented on the stories presented here. Their suggestions helped to improve the readability level of the stories. By name, they are Mary Brady, Debbie Eadens, Judy Goff, Kim Hoffman, Sandy Kearny, Bob Scantland, Diann Waddle, Rebecca Witt, Jackie Woods, and Lorenia Wright.

Introduction

This book contains eight scary stories. All of them are set in Kentucky, and all are told to be true. They tell about death and the return of the dead as spirits, or ghosts.

Many readers may think that ghosts are not real. People may only imagine that they see, hear, or feel them. Whether ghosts are real or not, someone you know may believe that they are real. The main thing to keep in mind as you read these stories is that they were told as truth. The ghosts were very real to those who saw or heard them.

Stories like the ones in this book are told by people all over the world. Every group has its own name for the spirits described in these scary tales. Here in Kentucky we mainly refer to them as "ghosts," "hants," or "haints." You will see all three words used in the stories. They all mean the same thing. They refer to the spirits of dead people or animals that have a strong urge to return to the land of the living. These ghosts sometimes come back to do evil. However, most of them return to aid or comfort old friends or relatives in need.

The stories you will be reading are a part of what is called folklore. This means that they were passed on by word of mouth from one generation to the next. Ghost stories have been told and passed on this way for hundreds of years and are still told today.

The tales in this book are based on real accounts told by Kentuckians from the 1930s to the present. Some stories were taken from my book called *Ghosts Along the Cumberland.* Others came directly by word of mouth. I have added details to make the stories more readable, but I was careful to retain the original core of each story. I had a purpose in making the stories longer. I wanted to give you a deeper insight into the lives of the Kentuckians who told these wonderful stories.

These accounts will also introduce the reader to the past. By describing old buildings and common events, they tell us much about local history and the way people lived back then. I also tried to make the reader hear the voices of the people who told these stories aloud.

While reading *Kentucky Ghosts,* keep two things in mind. First, the stories are rich in history. Second, they tell about spirits that were very real to the people who saw them or felt their presence. While you may not believe in ghosts, most likely one or more of your grandparents did. And they told stories about the ghosts in their lives.

I challenge you first of all to read *Kentucky Ghosts* to yourself. Then share the stories with your children or grandchildren, or the children who live around you. They'll enjoy them just as much as you do. Once you have read them, you may want to tell them to others. And, who knows, perhaps you will become a master storyteller as well as a fine reader.

Cries of a Dead Man

People around here used to tell old scary tales until bedtime. Wasn't anything else to do back in early times here in southern Adair County except sit around the stove or fireplace after supper and talk. People told stories about Indians, about the Civil War, about the old people in the family and community who were already dead, about witches, and about signs of death in the family. Most of all, though, they liked stories about ghosts. People called them "hant tales" back then.

These hant tales were filled with the different ways that ghosts made themselves known to people here in the world of the living. Dead children often visited their parents. Other dead family members sometimes came back to help their living relatives in one way or another. These spirits of the dead were often nothing more than ghostly lights or chilling breezes. At other times the spirits of the dead came back as headless beings. They would just stand in the middle of the road to await the coming of a wagon filled with young people on their way to a party. Many times, even the horses were scared of these road ghosts.

Some stories tell about headless spirits who lived in graveyards. Seems as if they just waited for a horse and rider to come by so they could hop on the back of the horse and wrap their boney arms around the rider's waist. Oh, I've heard them tell that story so many times.

But let me tell you a hant tale about the groans of a dying man who burned to death in an awful fire. This story scared the dickens out of me every time I heard my Grandmother tell it.

The setting for the story was back years ago. It was so long ago, in fact, that people then didn't even have coal oil for their lamps. They had to use candles to have light around the house. You couldn't see a thing without candles and not a whole lot with them! The candles made giant shadows on the walls. It was easy to imagine that ghosts and other scary things were in the room with you.

Even the wealthy families lived like this. This one rich family in Adair County built a big fancy house with huge hanging crystal lamps that sparkled in the candlelight. They wanted all these fine things so they could have lots of parties and dances.

One night this family was having a big dance—a ball, they called it. And all the well-to-do people were there from miles around. Well, along about 10 o'clock that night they were all dancing and having a good time. Suddenly, a man burst through the front door. He yelled in a loud voice, "Have you all heard about that murder that took place just across the state line over in Tennessee?"

Everybody stopped dancing the minute they heard him. One of the men called out to the fellow, "We've not heard anything. Tennessee is forty miles from here. How do you think we would have heard? What happened, anyway? Who was killed?"

The fellow, somewhat calmed down by then, said, "Well, there was a pretty, young girl murdered down there. The man who killed her got away, and they can't find him. They know who he was, but they can't locate him anywhere. The killer's hiding out somewhere, and the law officers think that he's in Kentucky, maybe even up here in Adair County at this very moment."

One of the ladies screamed out, "My God, no telling where he is! He might be right here in this very house ready to kill one of us!"

After awhile, everyone settled down a bit. Some of the dancers got to joking about the whole matter. But it wasn't long until things began to get out of hand. The fellows began teasing the young women by asking what they would do if the killer showed up and asked one of them to dance.

Finally, one of the fellows challenged the young

women by saying, "The bravest girl here will take a candle and go upstairs and look under the bed to see if the killer is hiding there."

The women were upset at the very thought. None of them wanted to do it. "Oh, no, no, no," they cried out.

But Mr. Bell, the owner of the mansion, stepped forward with a lighted candle and handed it to his daughter. He said to her, "There never was a Bell yet who was afraid of anything. Now, take that candle and go upstairs and look under the bed. If he's there, just call out and we'll all come running up to capture him."

She was shaking all over as she took the candle from her father's hands and slowly went up the creaking stairs. With trembling hands, she opened the door to her bedroom and stepped inside. Fear gripped her and chill bumps stood up on her arms. She sensed someone else there in the room with her. When she got up enough courage to lift the covers and look under the bed, the killer lay there staring back at her. She screamed aloud, dropped her candle, and fell to the floor in a faint.

Just as soon as the other dancers heard the scream, they grabbed up as many candles as they could find and headed upstairs to see what had happened. They found the girl there on the floor.

They took her downstairs and bathed her face in cold water until she came to.

Some of the men grabbed the killer and took him to the basement. There they tied him up with a rope. They decided they would turn him over to the law the next day. Everyone went back to dancing and making music. The party was still going strong well after midnight. In the excitement, no one knew that the girl had dropped her candle on the bed. While they danced, flames grew overhead.

The dancers were having fun and making so much noise that they didn't notice the house was on fire. The first they knew of it, the ceiling was about to cave in on them. People began screaming and running from the burning building.

The fire had already burned so much that it was impossible to save the house. No one thought of the killer tied up in the basement until it was too late to save him. As the crowd stood looking on in horror, the entire house caved in. They said that it was impossible to describe the moans and groans and cries and screams that came from the fellow's lips as he died there in that fire. People always claimed that the way he died didn't matter. They said he would have been hanged on the gallows for killing that girl over in Tennessee. Either way, there was no escape for him.

Now, that was a wood frame house that burned to the ground in the fire. The Bells were rich, so they replaced it with a fine brick home. Said it was one of the finest of its time. But wait till you hear the rest of the story.

I always heard that every night at about the same hour the man had burned to death in the basement of the old house, the Bell family could hear him moaning and groaning under their new house. Finally, the Bells couldn't take it any longer, so they sold the house and moved away. It was sold several times after that, as each new owner could also hear the ghostly moans and groans coming from the basement.

Just why, I don't know, but the Christian people of the community went together and bought the old brick building and tore it down. Using the brick from the house, they built a new church on the same spot. Even that didn't stop the ghostly cries and screams. It was said that they could still hear the man under that church building groaning every night.

Now that's the story of the ghostly moans and groans. And I reckon it was true from what I've always heard.

The Skeleton Under the Old Fireplace

I'm an old woman, so I've had a long lifetime to hear all kinds of ghost stories. I've heard stories about ghostly coffins with dead people in them floating across the room. And people like to tell about hearing ghostly cries and screams in houses, and of seeing ghost-like lights. I've even heard tell of someone dressing in front of a mirror and seeing the spirit of a dead person staring at them over their shoulder.

Let me tell you the story my Grandma used to tell about the night that the ghosts made all the chimney stones fall away from the house. It took place about 100 years ago, here in Lincoln County at my grandparents' old house. The house had a very large chimney. During pioneer times in Kentucky, many well-to-do families built houses with big chimneys. It is said that at one time my grandparents' house had one of the biggest stone chimneys ever seen on any house in central Kentucky.

My grandmother's name was Sarah Susan Wiley. Granddaddy's name was Joe Eagle Wiley. Oh, I loved to hear the two of them sit together and talk about the old times. They could tell some mighty good stories about ghosts and other things like that.

The first sign of ghost trouble, Granny said, occurred about a week after my grandparents moved into the big house they had just bought. It was winter, and they were sitting around the blazing fire talking about how good it felt to be in their cozy new home. They sure liked the huge fireplace with its wide hearthstone. Suddenly, the flame in the oil lamp fluttered as if a breeze had blown across the room. Indeed, it did feel like a breeze! But Grandmother claimed that all the windows and doors were closed to keep out the chill night air. It was strange, and they wondered how the draft had come in.

Next evening the two of them again sat around the fireplace. They talked about the day's work just ended and what they would do tomorrow. Suddenly, they heard a mournful sound coming from the area of the open fire. Grandmother gasped, then covered her mouth with the palm of her hand. The hairs on Granddaddy's arms stood straight out. They both felt a spirit present there in the room with them. With another puff of breeze, the unseen spirit left the room.

They sat up late, feeling uneasy, but nothing more happened. So Granddaddy banked the embers of the fire with ashes so that the coals would still be red in the morning. Then both of them climbed into their bed across the room from the fireplace.

About midnight, Grandmother awoke and sat right up in bed. She could see a strange light in the darkness there in front of the stone fireplace. Within the light she saw the figure of a woman dressed in black. She again cupped her hand to her mouth to smother a gasp. She saw the sad face of the ghost woman for only a moment. Then it faded away into the hearthstone that covered the floor in front of the fireplace. Grandmother's heart raced wildly.

Granddaddy sat up in bed, startled at the noise she had made. "What's wrong?" he wanted to know.

She told him of seeing a ghostly lady all dressed in black. He, too, shook from fear of the unknown and vowed to do something about it the very next day.

"Tell you what let's do," said Granddaddy. "We'll get Old Man Johnny Emberton to come stay in the house for a few weeks. That way we can go to Kansas and visit my brother, Frank. If anybody can handle a ghost, Old Man Emberton can. Everybody says that he knows how to talk to spirits."

Johnny Emberton seemed to attract ghosts. Since his wife had died, he had been moving from place to place, working for people by doing farm chores and odd jobs. He was known as an honest fellow with a special talent for speaking with spirits. He claimed that he learned how to do this from his dead wife. He had already made contact with various spirits by using a series of knocks on the wall. He knew to ask his questions so that they could be answered with either a "yes" or a "no." The spirits rapped on the wall three times if the answer was "yes," twice if "no." His questions were sometimes answered when the spirit appeared before him and used hand gestures or body movements to give its answers.

Well, Granddaddy and Grandma went off to Kansas as soon as they could make travel plans. Johnny Emberton moved into their house, ready to begin his job of awaiting the return of the ghost. He didn't know whether it would appear as a breeze, a spirit being, a ball of fire, a noise, or in some other form. Although the old fellow was not afraid, he did not look forward to meeting up with a new spirit being.

One day just before dusk, Emberton built a roaring fire in the fireplace. He sat looking out the window, wondering what would happen that night. He wasn't scared, but he was feeling tense over his chances of seeing a ghost. After all, no one can be calm and at peace when the spirit of a dead person is likely to appear.

Suddenly, Emberton leaped to his feet. Through the window he could see that something had come out of the old cemetery down the road and was headed toward the house. As the figure came closer, Emberton saw that it was a woman dressed in a white satin gown. She was holding the ends of a white shawl over her shoulders. The woman was not walking but floating along about a foot off the ground. It was a ghost! The old man's heart thumped in his chest.

Emberton watched as the spirit creature floated closer and closer to the house. Then it floated right through the closed door, just as if the door were not there. Appearing not to notice him, the lady ghost moved silently across the room. She went over and stood on the hearthstone in front of the old stone chimney.

Then another spirit dressed all in black rose up from the hearthstone and floated toward the woman in white. Sobs made by both ghosts broke the silence of the moment as they stood very close to each other, almost in an embrace.

Old Man Emberton finally got up enough courage to address the two spirits. The three of them talked to each other by tapping on the wall and by making a few hand signs. He learned that the spirit dressed in black was the earthly mother of the woman in white who had drifted down the road from the cemetery.

After seeing the ghosts of the two women, Emberton began to ask people around the neighborhood about the history of Granddaddy's property. He learned that the first family that lived there moved in about 1841. Their name was Banks, and they had built an old log house that was once located about a hundred yards down the road. The woman of the family had died in childbirth. Before her death she had made one final request. She asked to be buried close to the house so that she would never be very far away from her husband and children.

It seems that some rich neighbors bought the Banks farm. They built their new house in such a way that the stone chimney was located right on top of the woman's grave. It didn't matter to them that her remains had been buried there. After all, her corpse was six feet underground, and this was a beautiful spot for a house. It overlooked the grass-covered valley below.

The people who built the big house over the woman's grave decided to sell it after they had lived in it for only a few months. Their neighbors wondered why they were so eager to get rid of it. No one knew that the spirit of the dead woman dressed in black had scared them into moving out. Then my people came along. They knew nothing of the corpse whose burial spot had been disturbed. They didn't know that the big house with the large limestone chimney was built over a grave.

Old Man Johnny Emberton wrote to Grandfather

and Grandmother in Kansas and told them what had happened. He strongly urged them to tear away the fireplace completely and remove the hearthstone as well. But they never got the chance.

When they first got back home, Grandmother and Granddaddy were pretty nervous. Neither of them saw nor heard anything that first evening before going to bed. They were awakened in the middle of the night by a very loud noise that shook the entire house. They jumped out of bed and ran outside, not knowing what to expect.

They saw that the entire chimney had fallen down and lay in a pile just outside the building. When they came back inside, they saw that the heavy hearthstone, too, was broken into several pieces.

As they stood there scared and puzzled, a dim, ghostly light began to come from the fireplace hearth. Slowly, ever so slowly, it beamed up through the broken pieces of stone. Then, just as slowly as it had appeared, the light faded away.

Almost as if they were pulled in by the spirit, Grandmother and Granddaddy walked closer to the hearth. They dragged away one of the broken pieces of the heavy hearthstone. Underneath the rock was a human bone. When they removed other stones, they found more bones.

The spirit of the dead woman whose remains they had uncovered whispered to them from a dark corner of the room, "Bury me with my daughter and the rest of my family."

The very next day they buried her bones in the cemetery just down the road from the house. At last, she was with her loved ones. Granddaddy rebuilt the big stone chimney and hearthstone to their original glory. No breezes, nor noises, or any human spirits were ever felt or seen in or around the big fireplace after that.

Popular Foot,
the Dancing Road Haint

This county has never been remembered as a place
with good roads. County roads, where there were
any, always had deep ruts, mudholes, and big rocks
or stumps. There was always something in the way
to slow you down. But the roads that were haunted
by ghosts held the biggest surprises! My Granny
used to tell stories about the ghosts that haunted the
road by the Baptist church graveyard. Granny was a
Methodist, you know. But she never did believe the
stories that used to be told about a dancing ghost
called Popular Foot.

Popular Foot was a ghost without a head. He
used to haunt a section of the road between London
and Maplesville. He wasn't like a regular headless
ghost, the kind that would scare folks out of their
wits. In fact, Popular Foot, was, well, kind of
popular.

The story goes that he was the ghost of a
wandering fiddler. Back in those days old-time
fiddle players traveled the backroads in search of
work at dances. Sometimes they stayed in people's
homes and gave music lessons in exchange for a
few meals and a bed. One summer night this
fiddler left a dance real late. He was pretty tired

out, and he had been drinking a little too much. He lay down at the side of the road about a half mile from the farm where the dance was held. Soon he was sound asleep. Later that night, just before dawn, some boys who had been drinking even more than the fiddler came roaring down the road in a heavy wagon. They were shouting and whipping up the horses. The fiddler didn't hear them, even though they were pretty loud. He was passed out, dead asleep. Well, the wagon came rushing on down the dark road. The boys didn't see the fiddler lying there in the dark. The horses and that wagon ran right over him. One of the wheels cut off the poor man's head. He never knew what hit him.

The dance he had played at that night was at the Collins place. The family had five girls. When the Collins girls were young, they used to have a lot of dances. I believe that the fiddler was buried in the Collins family graveyard, just down the road. Since he was a wanderer, nobody knew where he was from or who his people were.

Of course, people talked about the fiddler for a long time. They wondered where he was from and if someone should try to find out who his family was. They talked about how shocking his death was and the evils of dancing and drinking liquor. I don't know, but I doubt if anyone ever found out anything about him. Then came the scary stories.

One time there was a man driving a wagon load of tobacco to market. When he got up around the Collins place he noticed the figure of a man walking along behind him. Said he looked just like a regular person, only he kind of glowed in the darkness, and he didn't have a head. I'll bet he put those mules into a run when he saw that headless man, rough road or not!

Popular Foot was seen quite often after that. Nobody was calling him Popular Foot yet, though. That came later. They just called him the Headless Haint. How he came by the name of Popular Foot is a different story.

As I said earlier, the Collins family had a lot of girls. They didn't have any dances for a while after the fiddler was killed. They waited until things calmed down. But it wasn't long before Lillie, the middle girl, and the next youngest, Alice, were of courting age. They were pretty fair looking, as Collins girls go. Anyway, Cy Collins was having a dance for Lillie's birthday. He had hired a fiddler from around Brock, named Billy Atwood. I believe he had a banjo player there, too.

Brock is a good six miles below here by way of London. Atwood did not have a horse. He could only get a ride part of the way, so he had to walk the last couple of miles to the Collins place. It was getting dark by the time he got that far, and he was tired. He sat down by the road to rest.

He had been resting for a few minutes when he noticed a strange figure coming up the road. As it came closer, Atwood could see that it was the Headless Haint. He had heard about the fate of the poor fiddler and knew better than to run. He believed he had an idea of what that poor ghost needed. So, when the ghost sat down next to him, Atwood pulled his fiddle and bow out of his pack and began to play a sad tune. He said to the ghost, "I'm sure Cy Collins didn't hire anyone to play at your funeral, ghost. I will play you a sad hymn, and perhaps that will set your spirit to rest."

"No, indeed, he did not," replied the ghost, "but it's not funeral music I care to hear. We dead folks can hear that any time. What I want to hear is a lively dance tune."

I'm sure I don't have to tell you that Atwood was awfully surprised to hear a headless ghost talk. His jaw must have dropped a foot. But after he got his mouth closed, he pulled the bow across the strings of the fiddle, a little rough at first. Then he slid right into a fine old dance tune.

The feet of the ghost began to shuffle a little with the rhythm as Atwood got into the heart of the song. Then it started to clap its hands. Atwood kept right on playing, seeing that the ghost was getting into the spirit of the music. In fact, in a moment that ghost jumped up and broke into a full jig, stomping high and swinging its arms!

Atwood played another tune, and the ghost kept right on dancing. After the second song, Atwood stopped.

"Ghost," he said, "you dance better than any dead man I have ever seen. You could beat some of the living ones, too. But I must get on to the dance."

"Thank you, fiddler," replied the ghost. "I do feel a bit more peaceful after hearing music again. You know, when you are the fiddler, you don't get to take your turn dancing. Don't let the night go by without getting a dance in yourself."

Atwood did not tell anyone at the Collins place about his run-in with the ghost. He never said a word about it to anyone until later that summer. That's when he came across Les Jenkins, a guitar player. They were both playing at a party down on the Laurel River, near Bert. It was hot, so they were taking a break, sitting outside to get some air.

"Billy," says Les, "Have you ever seen anything strange on the Maplesville road over by the Collins place?"

"Well," says Atwood, slowly, "what exactly do you mean?"

"They say that a fiddler was killed on the road there a few years ago. I think I might have seen him," replied Jenkins, looking his friend in the eye.

Billy Atwood smiled slowly. "Yes, I believe I have seen him. Did you notice how he likes to dance?"

It seems that the ghost got to know most of the musicians around the county. He didn't just hang out on the Maplesville Road waiting for someone to hold a dance around there. He started to show up all over that part of the county, wherever there was a party or music. It was almost as if he had his own special invitation. That was when people started to call him Popular Foot because he could dance so well and went to all the parties.

Mostly it was the musicians who saw him, coming or going from the job. They thought of him as their good luck charm, as though Popular Foot was looking after them in some way. Mike Christy, a banjo player, claimed that Popular Foot saved him from getting robbed one time.

There were some rough fellows running around the county then. They would steal your horse or your money if you came across them. Christy was riding home from visiting his folks when they came galloping up on him. As they got closer, Popular Foot suddenly appeared and told Mike to get down from his horse and play his banjo.

"But, Popular Foot, I don't have my banjo with me!" Mike said.

"That won't matter. You just play like you had one in your hands, and I will make the music and dance!"

So when the rascals came upon them, Christy was playing an invisible banjo that made real music for a headless dancer! Those bandits didn't even bother to get off of their horses. They only paused long enough to get a good look and kept right on going. They never were seen in that part of the county again.

Popular Foot has not been seen around here for a long time now. There aren't many parties and dances anymore. First there was the radio, then the picture show in London. Then they started working on the roads, getting the main ones paved for cars. Many of the old fiddle and banjo players are gone now, moved off or dead. I guess Popular Foot figured out that he wasn't needed anymore. But some folks around here still do remember him with a great deal of fondness.

The Granny Harris Story

My family always told ghost stories when I was a child back during the Great Depression years. That was in the 1930s. Times were hard then. We had very little money to buy things. After supper, sometimes we'd just sit around and tell those old scary stories until bedtime.

Seems as if every person on my father's side of the family had seen strange lights or heard ghostly moans and groans. I can't count the times that I've heard my Aunt Marie tell about things she had seen or heard. And there's Uncle Fred, Daddy's half-brother. He wasn't afraid of anything. If anything, a haint would run from *him*!

Our stories often told how dead family members came back as ghosts. It was always felt that the appearance of a spirit was meant to be a sign of something to come. That way, the family would know what to expect in the next few days. Maybe it would be the death of someone else in the family. Or perhaps it was just a sign that they could expect good news of some sort. People believed in such things back then. They even listened and watched for things to happen.

When I was a little boy, my great-grandmother was still alive. We all called her Granny. Granny was married to a man we called Pa Harris. He was Granny's second husband. Her first husband died back in 1892 while he was still a young man. I never knew him, but I do remember Pa Harris and all those old scary tales he told. Now there was a man who could tell about seeing and hearing all kinds of strange things! He believed in spirits, and his stories scared the daylights out of us kids every time we went to see him. Still, we always begged him to tell another one.

Some of Pa's stories told about the Simpson graveyard, which was less than half a mile from his and Granny's house. He always claimed that ghostly lights had been seen in that old graveyard. And he'd heard weird noises, too—the kind of moaning and groaning sounds that dead people make when their spirits cannot find rest.

I often walked the three miles from my house to see Pa and Granny Harris. My grandmother and two aunts also lived there with them in that big old two-story house. As a little fellow I was always afraid to go near the Simpson graveyard, afraid a "booger" would get me. That's another word we used in talking about ghosts.

There were only two roads I could walk along to get to Pa and Granny's house. Each one held out the chance of my running into haints.

One way was a private road that passed in front of Old Man Hacker Rich's house. It had been deserted for many years and was simply falling apart. Trouble was, the Old Hacker Rich house was full of ghosts. Whether real or imagined, to me there were spirit beings hanging from every rafter in that house. Eyes peered at me from every window, or so I thought.

The only other road that I could take ran right by the Simpson graveyard. That's the one I usually chose when I went alone to see Pa and Granny. I recall how scared I was of that old graveyard. It was bordered by tall cedar trees that could be seen from far away. There were many graves there. Some of them held the remains of people who died long before the Civil War. Cholera and typhoid fever had killed them. Other graves were those of Civil War soldiers who had been shot or hanged by their own neighbors. Little houses stood over some of the graves. People believed that these tiny buildings kept rainwater from reaching the bodies of the dead persons buried there.

I didn't hang around the graveyard very long. I was sure that if I did, I would hear the sounds and cries made by these people when they died. Each time I got within sight of this historic old graveyard, I began to whistle. My pace quickened. By the time I was alongside the graveyard, I always broke into a full run and ran the rest of the way. Neither Pa nor Granny or any of my other relatives ever asked why I was out of breath when I got to their house.

Granny had been sick for some time when I turned eight years old. Back then, people believed that when some part of the earth or sky acted in a strange manner, someone in the family or community was marked for death. I'll go ahead now and tell about the sudden appearance of 24 doves. See, these doves were a sign that Granny Harris would die.

As an 8-year-old, I had gone with my parents and my brother and sister to visit Granny. We often spent the night there, especially when Granny began to get weaker. This was in August. We had just finished eating supper, with lots of corn bread left over. All of a sudden, the gray doves flew onto the side porch and began pecking around as if they had come for a long visit. My 17-year-old Aunt Marie was Granny's youngest granddaughter. Aunt Marie took what was left of the corn bread and went onto the porch to feed the doves.

I watched through the window as she walked in the midst of the birds and crumbled the bread on the porch. The doves seemed tame and never moved away from her. Aunt Marie actually pushed the doves aside with her feet several times so as not to step on them. She came back into the house and calmly said, "Granny will die tonight."

None of the 8 or 10 people in the room asked her not to make such statements. The adults believed in such signs and watched for them, especially during periods of sickness.

At 4 o'clock the next morning, my father came to the bed where my brother and I lay sleeping. He shook us gently and said, "Wake up boys, Granny just died."

Granny was a wonderful woman. Everybody loved her and really missed her. The old homeplace was never quite the same again. Oh, some things were the same, because Granny's pictures and things still hung on the walls. And her furniture and dishes were still in the house for years to come. We all think that her spirit visited the old place at times until the house was finally sold and torn down in the 1960s. I've heard my mother and father talk about hearing strange noises. They thought the noises were made by Granny.

On one occasion they stayed all night there two or three years after Granny's death. Along about midnight or a little afterwards, something like the sound of pistol shots coming from the fireplace woke them up. They couldn't figure out where the noises came from. Then they heard something like a whisper or a breeze gently moving across the floor. They were a little scared, but not too afraid since they were there together.

Mama said that along about 1 o'clock the sewing machine began sewing. She said they heard the pedal moving just as clear as anything. She claimed they could hear scissors cutting through the cloth.

Mama said Daddy asked, "What in the world is Marie doing sewing this time of night?" They heard the sounds off and on all through the night.

Then early the next morning Aunt Marie came to Mama and Daddy's room and asked them, "Did you sleep okay last night?"

"No," both of them answered her at the same time. "Why in the world did you need to sew all night on that sewing machine?" Daddy asked her.

Marie told them that she hadn't been sewing. Then she went on to say that she knew who it was. Marie said that along about 3 o'clock in the morning she couldn't stand the suspense any longer. She got up and went upstairs to the workroom. Granny was sitting there in front of the machine, just working away. On her lap was the dress she had been making when she got sick.

Marie told of other visits by Granny's spirit, but she was never afraid when she saw her. She claimed that Granny's visits were of a peaceful nature, just as she was when she was alive. But let me finish talking about Granny Harris by telling about her and the Union soldiers, and then how she came back to save my Daddy from sure death. Both of these things took place at the same spot.

Granny was confronted by these Union soldiers when she was only 5 years old. It had been her job each afternoon to go into the pasture field to find the cows and drive them to the barn to be milked.

On one summer day during Civil War times, Granny had gone to get the cows. She stopped to rest for a moment under a very large white oak tree. Some of the tree roots were above ground, making a seat. Granny sat down on one of the big roots. She threw her head back and began to sing at the top of her voice. She thought that only the cows would hear her!

Suddenly, a bunch of Union soldiers stepped from behind the bushes. "Sing that song again, little girl," one of them ordered her.

She was scared to death, but did sing the song for them. Then she watched as they left her standing under the big oak tree and headed out across the field to rob her family's smokehouse.

Across the years, that old oak tree stood as a landmark. By 1945, it was dead and in its final stages of decay. That was the year that my Daddy bought a load of corn from a nearby farmer. He was hauling it home in a horse drawn wagon. The road on which he was traveling passed right by the big oak tree. As Daddy neared the big tree, he became somewhat uneasy. He even asked himself if it would be safe to travel under the big oak. It just might fall on him.

As he got closer to the old tree, his horses began to act very strange. They came to a sudden stop, lunged first to the left and then the right. One of the animals reared up to the point that both front feet were off the ground. Daddy said that by that time he was scared to death. He didn't know what to do.

Then he saw a likeness of Granny emerge from behind the tree. She walked across the road in front of him, smiled, and motioned him to stop by holding up her hands.

Then Granny's spirit slowly faded out of sight. Daddy heard loud cracking noises. Suddenly, the old oak tree fell to the ground right across the road in front of his wagon. If Granny had not been there to warn him, Daddy would have been killed that very instant.

He's told me that story so many times. And I firmly believe it, too.

Dog Ghost Seeks Revenge

There's a lot of old folk beliefs about dogs and the way they act. I recall hearing people talk about these things when I was a little fellow. For sure, my relatives here in Trigg County, now the Land Between the Lakes, believed that certain actions of dogs were signs of things that were about to happen. Some of these signs were good, others not so good.

I've heard people in the community say that if you hear dogs howling late at night in an eerie, mournful way, a death in the family is sure to follow. Some said, too, if dogs howl when someone is seriously sick, that person will die soon. Now don't laugh when I tell you this one, but they always claimed that when a dog rolls over on its back and lies still, you'll hear of a death in the community.

Years ago we had an old dog named Bravo. He proved to me that these beliefs weren't all nonsense. Bravo wasn't a house dog. Truth of the matter is, you couldn't get him in the house! He would come onto the porch, but all the tugging in the world wouldn't get him into the house. Well, late one afternoon my brother and I were out walking. Of course, Bravo was right there with us. We came by Old Man Miller's house. The poor fellow had been sick for some time. The door to his front room was open. And, do you know, Bravo went into that room and walked on over to Old Man Miller's bed.

The old fellow reached out and patted Bravo on the head. After a few minutes, the dog turned away and ran out of the room. He went out into the yard, lay down on the grass, rolled over, and stuck his feet and legs straight up into the air. My brother looked at me kinda funny. I knew right then what he was thinking. Sure enough, Old Man Miller died that night.

The strangest dog story I ever heard was about a ghost dog. The story centers on a man whose name was Ned Crawford. He killed a man and his dog over here in the Golden Pond community. Crawford always played a lot of cards and sometimes drank too much whiskey. Well, one night Crawford got into a fight during a card game with Paul Jackson, a neighbor who always took his black dog along with him. They were alone when it happened, at Jackson's lonely cabin.

No sooner had the fuss started before Ned pulled his knife and stabbed Jackson in the gut. As Jackson pitched backward the black dog snarled and jumped. It grabbed hold of Ned's free arm. He swung at the dog with his knife and cut the animal's throat. Blood from both victims covered the floor.

Crawford was panting and sweating. He had

done murder, and he was scared to death. All he could think to do was to take the two bodies to a muddy pond not far away. In the cover of darkness he dragged the bodies to the water and threw them in.

From that time on, Ned could never go anyplace without seeing the ghost of Jackson and his dog. Said he couldn't even step into his yard without seeing them. This ghost dog would come over to Crawford and just growl and grit its teeth at him.

Crawford was so scared that he finally left the county and went all the way to Springfield, Missouri. He figured he could start life all over there without anyone being suspicious. Crawford also thought that by moving away from the scene of the murder, he would get rid of the ghosts of Jackson and the dog. But the second night he was there in Missouri, he stepped into the yard of the house where he was staying. And, do you know, that dog was walking right along behind, just a few feet away.

This same thing took place almost every night for about three months. It just about worried Crawford to death. Sometimes, Jackson's ghost was there also. You see, Ned was feeling guilty over killing the man and his dog. He couldn't live with himself, and he couldn't stay there in Missouri any longer. He didn't know what else to do, so he came on back to his old home here in Kentucky.

Let me tell you right now, Ned Crawford was never himself again. He moved in with his mother, but she died soon after he got home. From what I hear, she must have worried herself to death over Ned's behavior, for he became very withdrawn. He hardly talked at all. She may not have known what he had done, but she must have known that it was something bad.

After his mother's death, the only thing Crawford would do was go down to the general store. He would just sit there on a nail keg. He never would say a word to any of the rest of us. We all wondered why he wouldn't talk. He had always gone to the store as a boy to drink cold sodas and eat peanuts and cheese and crackers with the other boys. Back then he talked as much as the rest of us.

Anyway, an older fellow there at the store asked Crawford to go home with him. This man's name was Willie Smith. He said he needed help with harvesting the wheat crop. Smith even invited Crawford to eat his meals with them and spend the nights there. Crawford still didn't say a word; just followed Smith home.

When they got there, Willy Smith suggested that the two of them go for a ride on horseback. It was a fine late summer evening, and there was plenty of time before supper. Smith saddled up two horses, and they went riding off down the road, not far from the pond where Crawford had tossed the bodies of Jackson and his dog.

Well, lo and behold, a big black dog appeared suddenly and just stood there in the middle of the road in front of Smith and Crawford. The ghost dog's eyes were shining something awful, and its teeth gleamed as it snarled at Crawford. Then the dog turned away and headed toward the pond. It walked right into the water and disappeared. Soon, the dog came out of the pond with a bone in its mouth.

The dog, or I should say the ghost of the dog, came up to the two men and dropped the bone right at their feet. "Thud," it went as it hit the ground. The reins shook in Crawford's hands, but he didn't say a word.

Smith didn't know what to make of what he saw. He knew that something strange was going on because the bone didn't look like a hog or cow bone. It looked like a human bone. Smith knew right then that the dog was trying to tell him something.

Crawford sank down in the saddle and placed his head in his hands. He began to cry and shake all over. It was then that he admitted killing Paul Jackson and his big black dog. He claimed that he couldn't shake the memory of the awful thing he had done. He went on to tell how he had seen the ghosts of both Jackson and his dog for months every time he stepped out of the house.

Smith got down off his horse and pulled Crawford out of the saddle. He took Crawford by the arm and led him over to the edge of the pond. The ghost of the big black dog stood a few feet away and watched as Smith pulled more bones from the pond.

Crawford was turned over to the sheriff and put in jail to await trial for murder. The jury convicted him of the crime, and the judge gave him a lifetime in prison for what he had done. But neither the judge nor any of the others present in the courtroom that day witnessed what Crawford saw at that very moment. Nor could they understand his great sigh of relief.

The big black dog's ghost had been standing in the doorway of the courtroom, visible only to Crawford. When the dog ghost heard the judge proclaim Crawford's life sentence, it turned around and slowly faded away in a faint cloud of mist. Crawford smiled. Although he faced a prison cell for the rest of his life, he knew that he would never again see the dog or its master.

The ghost of a dog had seen justice done.

Bloodstains on Top of the Well

Hollis Thompson told me an interesting story. It was about a bloodstain on the water well at this old house his family moved into back in 1943. That was right in the middle of World War II. Hollis said that he was just a 5-year-old boy at the time.

The house into which the Thompsons moved was very old. As a matter of fact, the house was so run-down that it had to have a lot of repair work done before they moved in. I've heard Hollis say that there was no overhead ceiling upstairs. The ceiling rafters had been handmade. The axe marks made in them many years ago were still visible. He told me many other things about that house and all the old outbuildings around it. Let me tell you right now, a lot of his stories were scary. But there was one story about the old plank-covered well that really scared me. It made my blood turn cold every time I thought of it, especially after dark.

The story had its beginnings around 1900. Back then, a Russell family owned the farm there and lived in the house. They liked to have parties and always invited their friends and neighbors in to have a good time with them. One night the Russell family held a corn shucking party in the house. That's a party people had back then as a way of getting their corn shucked. They could have a barrel of fun doing it. Fellows always liked these parties. Every time one of them found a red ear of corn, he got to kiss the girl of his choice.

Well, it just so happens that the Russells were also the parents of the prettiest girl for miles around. Her name was Katy. She was engaged to the toughest, meanest bully in three counties. Why she chose him I'll never know. His name was Wayne Babbit. People claimed that he stole chickens and hams of meat from his neighbors. If they said anything about it, he always pulled a gun out of his pocket and flashed it at them. Babbit wouldn't work on his own farm. As a matter of fact, he mainly just rode his horse up and down the road. People always said that he was just a troublemaker.

Later in the evening the corn shucking was about over. The young, single people began playing a game called "Pleased or Displeased." One of the men asked Josh Cook, a younger brother of Jim Cook, if he was pleased or displeased.

Josh told him that he was displeased.

"What would it take to please you?" the man asked.

Josh answered, "To see Katy kiss my brother Jim."

That statement tells me how much Josh wanted to see Katy marry Jim. He didn't like Babbit at all. And, too, Jim and Katy had been sweethearts at one time.

Jim had no choice in the matter but to do what Josh asked him to do. He took Katy in his arms and kissed her for what must have been a long time. This broke the game up, and in a few minutes people began to go home.

Wayne Babbit was very angry. When Jim and Josh Cook left the Russell house, he followed them outside. So did Katy. Jim and Babbit began to fight. The jealous Babbit took out his pocket knife. It was the kind they always called a razor knife. He opened the long shiny blade and made a dive for Jim Cook.

Suddenly, a woman's scream was heard by the people inside the house. The men all ran in the direction from which the scream had come. They found Katy standing by Jim Cook's body, which lay stretched out across the top of the old well. His head was gone. It had been totally cut off. There it was on the ground, eyes open and staring into the stillness of the cold, dark sky. Cook's blood had gushed out of his body and was all over the wooden planks that covered the well. It was an awful thing to see.

After the killing, Babbit ran and hid in the barn. The others found him there still holding the long, bloody knife blade in his hand. He denied killing Cook, but was soon tried and convicted of murder.

Katy never got over that awful event. She remained an old maid for the rest of her life.

The Russells never removed the old planks from the well top on which Jim Cook had been killed. The bloody spots could always be seen, especially after each rain. I guess that old folk belief is true. You know, the one that says the blood of a murdered person will always stain the spot where the killing took place.

Let's not forget that the Thompsons are a part of the story, too. Hollis and his parents moved into the Russell house when he was still a boy. It was early in the winter of 1943, and a few snows had already fallen. The winter's supply of wood was stored out back in the old woodshed near the blood-stained planks that covered the well. Hollis would walk by those blood stains and think of that terrible murder every time his mother sent him to get more wood for the fire. Hollis always claimed that the dancing shadows on the wall cast by the light from the fireplace made him think that great goblins would get him at just about any moment.

One night without warning, the weird, scary sounds began. It was about 8 o'clock in the evening when the Thompsons heard noises coming from the upstairs area. Something was pecking and banging on the old ceiling rafters. At first they thought it was only a rat, or perhaps a bird that had gotten into the house. The longer it went on, the louder it got. Finally, it sounded like a dog playing with a ball.

There was no such thing as electric power up in that hollow where they lived. They used kerosene lamps back then. With some hesitation, Hollis's father picked up a lamp with one hand and reached for his gun with the other. He began to move slowly toward the door that led upstairs. He walked ever so softly so as not to disturb whatever was making the noise. Suddenly, Thompson sprang forward, exposing himself fully at the bottom of the stairway. The lamp fluttered and the flame died for a second, then burned again. Only moments before, the upstairs area had been full of loud noises. But now there was only a deathly silence up there. Shaking his head in disbelief, Thompson returned to his chair in the living room.

None of the Thompsons said a word. I guess they were too scared to talk. It wasn't more than five minutes until the noise began again. This time, it was louder than ever. Hollis claimed that it sounded to him like a yearling calf romping and stomping.

Again, his father crept toward the base of the

stairs. He was even more careful this time not to be heard. When he flung himself into the stair opening, the sounds again stopped. Thompson came on back and took his chair. They heard nothing else that night, and the family finally went to bed.

The same noises continued night after night. The Thompsons never told anyone else. People might laugh at them for believing in such things.

One night about two months later, three friends dropped by the Thompson house. They were soldiers, friends of Mr. Thompson who were home on leave from the army. They were sitting around the fire talking with Mr. Thompson. The noises began again, very quietly at first. They were not even noticed by the three visitors. Soon, however, their ears perked up, and they began to ask what the noises were. Thompson avoided their questions as long as he could, but finally broke down and described all that had taken place. He told them about Jim Cook's death, and of the blood stains on the well.

The three fellows had a good laugh at Thompson's expense. All the while, he just sat there and didn't say a word. Within a few moments their joking stopped. They didn't utter a sound as they sat there listening to the noise. Every time they looked upstairs, trying to find the cause of the noise, it always stopped. I've often wondered if they stayed the rest of the night because they were curious or because they were too scared to go home.

When they left the next morning, one of the men turned to Thompson and said, "My friend, when you move from this house, I'll come back to see you and your family. But I'll never be back until you do."

The Thompsons continued to live in that old house for another two years. They were too poor, I guess, to go anyplace else. They set traps, put out poison, brought in cats, dogs, and weasels. They had hoped to catch whatever it was that made the noise. They nailed everything down on that house that might squeak or flap in the wind, and did whatever else they could think to do. Nothing worked. Hollis told me that his parents truly believed Jim Cook's spirit was living inside the house.

The Thompsons sold the place at a heavy loss in 1946. They packed up their things and very thankfully moved out of the hollow. To this day, Hollis maintains that he is not going back to visit anytime soon. And I don't blame him. I wouldn't either.

The Little Girl Ghost Who Adopted Us

The house that my family lived in looked pretty much the same as a lot of other country houses in Kentucky. When it was painted, which wasn't real often, it was white. There was a big front porch, and, inside, it was a regular farmhouse. Two rooms were downstairs, kitchen on the right and sitting room on the left. There were two bedrooms upstairs.

No one lives in that old house now. My folks, the Halleys, bought the house and farm about 1920, just after the First World War. Me and my wife Addie had a new brick house built a few years ago, just down the hill from the old place. We were glad to move into our new house for a lot of reasons. Some of the people in this community think we moved out of the old place because it was haunted.

Now I'm not the sort of person who scares easily. Ever since I was a small boy I have seen and heard many strange things in that house. They were strange things I never could explain. I don't have to prove that to anyone. I know what I saw and heard in that house was real.

My father bought that house from a family

called Pearson. The Pearsons had a little girl who had eaten a whole lot of walnuts that had laid out all winter and sprouted. She took sick and died in the house. A few people in my family have actually seen her ghost.

The first time anything happened was back when I was a little boy, in the late 1920s. For a while, every evening and every morning there came a knocking at the door. When someone opened it, no one would be there. I don't really remember that, but my dad used to talk about it. My mother nearly went crazy over it, because the knocking would just keep on until someone went to the door.

After that, things were quiet for a while. That little ghost must have gotten into the house one of those times when we answered the door. Before we knew it, we were hearing footsteps upstairs. We all heard them from time to time. Sometimes we heard them while we were at the dinner table, and we knew no one was upstairs. We would stop for a minute and listen. My dad did not want us to pay too much attention to it. I guess he thought we would be afraid, so he would start to talk about something else. Mother tried to join the conversation, but she always sounded tense. Then she would fall silent and look down, and sometimes close her eyes. Even though I was little, I knew she was praying.

Next to the door-knocking, the footsteps bothered Mother most. She told Dad that she often heard the steps when she was home alone, but she did not tell us kids. One day she couldn't stand it anymore. Mother had heard that if you asked the ghost what in God's name did it want, it would quit bothering you. That day when she was alone in the kitchen, she heard it walking directly overhead.

Gathering her courage, Mother shouted at the top of her lungs: "What in the name of God do you want?!" The footsteps instantly stopped, and she never heard them again when she was alone.

But that was not the end of our ghost. Over the years we got kind of used to seeing and hearing strange things. I remember the rocker in the sitting room, especially. Sometimes when you walked by the door to that room, out of the corner of your eye you would notice the rocking chair moving all by itself. It rocked slowly. It happened in the daytime when nobody was in the room, and even sometimes at night, when we were in there listening to the radio. We still heard the footsteps too, from time to time.

A cousin of mine, Sally, stayed with us for a few years when I was in my early teens. Once in a while Sally said she heard a sound from upstairs, a kind of humming, like a sewing machine. Every time she went up to find out what was causing the noise, she couldn't find a thing. Once when Sally went up to look, she locked the front door first. She was quite certain that it couldn't sneak out that way. Of course, she still didn't find anything.

Mr. Sanders, an old neighbor of ours, told me about the time he saw our little girl ghost. He said that one day he was riding by our house when he decided to stop in to say hello. As he rode his horse up to the house, he saw a little girl through the window. She was playing by herself near the fireplace. Sanders thought it was strange right off, because she did not look like anyone in our family, and it seemed that nobody was home. He went around to the back door to go in and speak to the child. But when he came inside he could not find her, although he searched the house.

As I said before, the little girl ghost took a special liking to my mother, who also saw her once. It was after Father had died. Addie and I had married and started our family, and we decided to stay on the family farm and live there in that old house. Mother stayed with us.

One day Mother was coming home from town. A friend dropped her off at the house. As she came up to the door, she also saw a little girl playing through the window. At that moment she didn't think much of it because she thought it was my daughter, Missy. But when she got in the house she saw that my wife, Addie, and little Missy were out in the garden patch. She got spooked then and ran out of the house calling them. Mother was breathless when she got to the garden patch and told them what she had seen.

Maybe you can get used to some things, even mysterious footsteps and such. But there were things that happened in that house that nobody could get used to, or forget.

One night about 9 o'clock I was upstairs in bed. Addie was gone with the baby to visit her sister. Anyway, I heard someone come across the front porch, enter the house, and come upstairs. Something walked across the floor and sat down on the bed beside me. I thought it was Addie, although I had no idea why she would come home so suddenly, so late at night. I reached with my hand and felt for her, but nobody was there.

Just then Mother, who slept downstairs, yelled up the steps and asked who it was. I said it wasn't anybody.

She said, "Well, I know it is. I heard someone." I got up and ran downstairs to get a light. Then I went back up there and searched the place over, but I didn't find a thing. Next day I moved Addie's and my bed into the other room upstairs. The ghost could have our room—we didn't need it that bad.

That was a good twenty years ago, and we have heard from the ghost off and on since then. But it was most active when there were children in the house, and ours are long since grown. I wondered if it would follow us when we built the new house, since it is just down the hill from the old one. But, thankfully, we have not seen or heard it since we moved. I don't miss it one bit.

How Otto's Ghost Saved Us from a Haunted House

I don't know why anyone would want to live on a farm when they were not raised to it. But when our children were little, my husband Jack and I were determined to get out of town and buy ourselves a farm. Every weekend we would check the ads in the newspaper and go out driving around the back roads of Muhlenberg County looking for just the right place. We both wanted a big, old farmhouse with a huge front porch and a fireplace inside. I wanted a yard with lots of big trees and flower beds and shrubs. Jack was looking for sturdy barns and sheds and a good tobacco base.

Of course, we looked at a lot of places, many of which had old houses on them. Sometimes when we went inside to look at one I would get a funny feeling, like there was someone in the room with us, only I couldn't see anyone. Jack would laugh at me. "We had better be careful," he said, "or we may buy ourselves a haunted house."

October came, and we still had not found a farm to suit us that we could afford. We decided to quit looking until the next spring. The house we were renting at that time was a small, three-bedroom brick structure. It had been built in the 1880s and still had an old coal furnace. The weather began to turn colder, and, since Jack was working nights, he decided to get someone to help keep the furnace running. Mrs. Shell, our neighbor, said that a fellow named Otto Callie had always taken care of her furnace and was a kind and reliable man. She sent Otto over to us a few days later. I liked him from the first moment I saw him.

Otto was in his late sixties, a black man with white, curly hair. When I asked him in to show him the furnace, he looked around at the house and smiled. "My Daddy helped to build this house," he told me. "He always had a special feeling about this place because it was the first house he ever worked on. His daddy, my grandfather, taught him how to lay brick, and they built this house together."

Every morning that winter Otto came to fire the furnace. The sound of his heavy footsteps on the cellar stairs, regular as clockwork, would awaken me at 5 o'clock every morning. After I heard him leave I would get up to start breakfast, for I knew Jack would be home soon.

On Mondays, Otto would come back for coffee around 9 o'clock, after he had finished his work. "Otto is here! Otto is here!" the children would call out when they saw him coming. They would jump around him, tugging on his sooty clothes, yelling, "Tell us a story, Otto, please!"

He would sit in the kitchen sipping his coffee and telling the children stories about clever B'rer Rabbit and Aunt Nancy the spider. His voice would change to fit each character, and he would wave his arms and stamp his feet in just the right places to show what he meant. I always enjoyed his visits and stories as much as the children did.

One Monday morning it was very dark and rainy, and the wind was blowing fearsome. Otto came in later than usual. He was wet and looked mighty tired. He groaned as he sat roughly down on the slat-back chair. "Are you feeling poorly today Otto?" I asked him.

"I am getting mighty old," he said, "I'm just feeling so tired. This weather puts demons in my bones so that I can't move."

"Real demons, Otto?" asked 6-year-old Ned. "Can you tell us a story about real demons, or maybe ghosts?" Ned pleaded.

"Ned," said Otto, "when you get as old as me you don't tell no ghost or demon stories because you are too close to Heaven and you don't want to make no trouble."

"Otto, is that where B'rer Rabbit is now, in Heaven?" Ned asked.

"No," replied Otto. "I expect B'rer Rabbit is too smart to die."

Not long after that, Otto was in the hospital. He had a heart attack while firing Mrs. Shell's furnace. He was not recovering, and the doctor said he only had a short time to live. I tried visiting him on Monday mornings, just like we used to. But he was very weak, so the doctor asked me keep it short. The last time I saw Otto he said, "You don't have to bother coming to see me again, Miss Jean. I will be gone by next Monday." And he died the following Sunday.

Jack, the children, and I attended the funeral. Even though we had known Otto only a short time, we really missed him. I even missed the way his footsteps on the cellar steps would awaken me in the morning. The winter passed on, a little more drab without Otto's stories.

When spring came, we resumed our search for a farm. One day when we were out driving the county roads we came across a lovely looking place. It had an old two-story frame house set among a grove of oaks and magnolias. "Look at this place, Jack. It's so pretty!" I said.

"We're in luck," Jack replied. "There's a 'For Sale' sign in front of it."

We decided to wait and call the realtor and get more information and an appointment to see the place instead of just dropping in on the owner. That was on a Sunday, and we could not get in to see the house until the next weekend. I was very excited, and I thought about it all week.

I tried to hide my excitement from Jack. He was taking a more practical approach to the matter.

"We have to see what the rest of the property is like, even if the house is nice," he reminded me.

The night before we went to see the house, I slept poorly and had a very strange dream. I dreamed that I was inside that farmhouse and could see each room very clearly. When I got to the bathroom, I saw that the walls were covered with bright pink tile. Then in my dream I heard Otto's voice saying, "Stay away from this house, Jean! It is an evil place!" When I awoke, I heard those footsteps on the cellar stairs, Otto's footsteps, at 5 o'clock, just when he used to come.

"Jack! Jack!" I shook my husband until his eyes opened.

"Jean, what is it?" Jack asked.

I told him of my dream and of hearing Otto's footsteps. His eyes opened wide as I spoke. I could see that he was a little uneasy, but he said nothing.

The next day we were both silent as we followed the realtor out to see the house. An old woman was living there. We asked her about the history of the house. "Oh, its very old," she said. "All of my husband's family have died here. I do believe it is haunted," she added in a soft voice.

As she showed us around the house, a sense of dread filled me. Everything was so familiar, as if I had been there before. Then she showed us the downstairs bathroom. The walls were covered in *bright pink tile*. Jack looked at me, then at the realtor. "I think we have seen enough," he said. We headed toward the door.

Puzzled, the realtor asked, "Are you sure you don't want to see the barn?" We stepped outside into the sunshine.

"We can't buy any houses with pink bathrooms," Jack said. The realtor gave us a look like we were crazy.

"I'll keep that in mind," he said.

When I went to bed that night, I said my prayers, just like I used to when I was a little girl. I said one just for Otto. I never did hear Otto's steps again, and we did finally find a farm that suited us, house and all—with a *blue* bathroom.

About the Author

William Lynwood Montell was born and grew up in north central Monroe County at a time when family storytelling was still very common. He liked hearing about the ghosts of past generations. His formal education began in a one-room school at Rock Bridge and ended at Indiana University where he received a Ph.D. degree in 1964.

Dr. Montell served as teacher and academic dean at Campbellsville College until 1969. He then moved to Western Kentucky University where he has taught folklore, folklife, history, and oral history classes and has served as a department head and assistant dean. He is widely known as the author of many books and journal articles that are based on local life and history. As you read the Granny Harris story in this book, you'll meet his great-grandmother, whom he knew and loved as a lad.